Stories 4 Women

A collection of true short stories

Amy Higgins Artino, Ashley M. Ratcliff,
Mary Scott, and Rebecca Villaneda

authorHOUSE®

AuthorHouse™
1663 Liberty Drive
Bloomington, IN 47403
www.authorhouse.com
Phone: 1-800-839-8640

First published by AuthorHouse 10/23/2010

ISBN: 978-1-4520-8460-2 (hc)
ISBN: 978-1-4520-8461-9 (sc)
ISBN: 978-1-4520-8462-6 (e)

Library of Congress Control Number: 2010914367

Printed in the United States of America

This book is printed on acid-free paper.

Acknowledgement

We dedicate this, our first book, to our loving families and wonderful friends — including our four-legged ones. Thank you for your support and encouragement.

We also would like to thank photographer Tom Underhill and editor Chris Boyd for their help with this book.

Introduction

As journalists we understand the importance of documenting the human condition. As women we feel it's just as important to share the experiences that unite us as a gender.

Yes, we've come a long way, but we still have further to go. Discrimination and sexual assault continue and we must not only come to terms with it but also stop it. Through the love of family and friends, and through the lessons of those who have come before us, we live through the trials and progress in an understanding that we are valuable. As a sisterhood, we clasp hands, hold on to one another and lift each other up in life.

The four of us are of different ages, come from different races and backgrounds, and have different political and religious views. Our perspectives may vary, but our individual stories resonate with each other. Collectively they encompass the experiences and emotions of womanhood — the obsession of teenage crushes, our complicated and loving relationships with men, our need for our mothers' nurturing care, dealing with tragedy and trauma, gaining independence, and realizing personal growth.

These stories explore our pain and sorrow, and delight in our joy and sense of humor. These stories are for women.

Table of Contents

Part I: Younger days 1

Chance made us sisters 3
Recipe for love.. 9
Thank heaven for him 17
A whirlwind first crush..23

Part II: Growing 33

Full circle... 35
My own.. 43
And don't call me 'Girly' 47
It's strictly platonic 53

Part III: Worst nightmare 59

Dislodging the demons... 61
A forgettable night..68

Part IV: Who we are 73

Independent bliss... 75
Making two worlds one 80
Journey to 'ever after'... 85
The agony of aging, the thrill of defeating it 92

Part I:
Younger days

Chance made us sisters

By Amy Higgins Artino

Three weeks after my second birthday, my parents brought home to me a baby sister. I was far less than thrilled. Being an only child and a Taurus, I didn't adjust well to change. I still often don't.

When she was alive, my maternal grandmother would tell me the story of the day my mother gave birth to Sara Kate, my sister. I was under my grandparents' care in New Jersey, just a short distance from Kennedy Memorial Hospital, where all of us grandchildren were born. My grandfather helped found the hospital, where he taught, and he practiced obstetrics and gynecology for many more years thereafter.

Nonna said I stood at the screen door and stared out, longing for my mother. Of the few words I uttered, the most prominent she heard were, "I hate that new baby, God damnit." Yes, I was a feisty toddler.

From that day on, all I knew was that this tiny being I didn't ask for came into our house and took my parents' attention away. (Looking back now, 27 years later, this seems so ridiculous.) It became my life's purpose to get rid of my little sister so I could have my parents back, all to myself.

One uncle likes to tell the story of the time Sara was asleep in a playpen at my grandparents' house. I attempted to climb into it so I could poke her in the eye until I woke her up, making her cry. Caught red-handed, my mother scolded me and asked me what I thought I was doing. I told her I was sick of this baby, and so I was renaming her Sara Fart. At the time, "fart" was the most heinous cuss word I could think of, as I got yelled at any time I said it. Having heard many grown-ups say "God damnit" when they were mad made me think saying that was OK.

The years went on, and I continued to torment my sister. The older we got, the more I hated her, especially since she got smart, knew I was more likely than she was to get in trouble and then used that to her advantage.

Take, for instance, the time I had my first Barbie, regaled in her peaches-and-cream ball gown with matching shoes and boa. It was the dress of all little girls' dreams: a fluffy, ruffly, peach-colored skirt with a white, iridescent bodice. It was divine. And Sara wanted her doll to wear it. The nerve! She told me if I didn't give it to her, she would bite herself on the arm and tell Mom that I did it so I would get in trouble. Pure evil, I tell you.

Plus, she was the baby, so she always got away with murder, while I always was the scapegoat.

Besides — she always was copying me! Everything I liked or wanted, she loved and had to have, too. And while I had to wait until I was 8 to get my ears pierced, she had hers done at the same time, though she was only 6. It was totally, utterly unfair.

There was another time, on her third birthday, when we were playing outside in my grandparents' vast yard. I found a piece of tinsel that must have gotten trapped in a bush after Christmas five months prior, and — as with all things shiny — we delighted in it.

"Let me have it!" she said, breathless with desire.

I looked her in the eye and promptly threw it away.

"Oops," I said.

She cried, and I had a little victory party in my head.

As the years went on, I ended up becoming a choir-and-theater geek in school, while Sara dressed all in black and hung out with the weirdo art kids. She listened to The Cure, Rage Against the Machine and Radiohead, while I preferred the divas of the music industry — Celine Dion, Janet Jackson and Mariah Carey — as I worked to perfect my soprano singing voice and grow as a songwriter. It all only served to underscore our differences, which multiplied as we got older.

Before too long, I was off to college, and I didn't see my sister as much because we no longer lived under the same roof. The times we did spend together seemed more friendly, as we had more to talk about and absence made our hearts grow fonder.

Two years after I started at the university, she was off to an exclusive, all-girls art-and-design school in center city Philadelphia to study fashion. I went with my parents the day she moved into her dorm. It was an unimaginably small room — you almost couldn't fit a single bed in there long-ways — in a building that at one time, we'd been told, was an insane asylum. Yikes! It was as if the inner demons of the edifice still lingered in the creepy hallways and shadows inside, with flickering, fluorescent lights and an eerie quiet that was unsettling. The institution itself is more than 150 years old.

When Sara's stuff was inside the room and we were all

standing out by the car preparing to leave her behind, we saw a group of students walk by. One girl, dressed in nothing other than yellow "Caution" tape from head to toe, walked among other girls with so many piercings in their faces that they looked like pin cushions. It was then that Sara appeared to me with the utmost clarity: She was my beautiful, fragile little sister, and we were about to leave her here with all those metal-punctured crazies in a converted nuthouse. I broke down.

"Mom, do we really have to leave her here?!" I sobbed.

From that point on, something shifted deep inside of me.

I saw my sister as someone I was chosen to protect, to look after and to set an example for. We weren't in competition — we were on the same team.

All those years I shunned, made fun of and tortured her came crashing down on me in one instant. I was shattered.

How in the world could I have been so cruel?

She didn't want to take my parents away from me; she was simply a gift who added to the family circle. She wasn't trying to steal my identity by copying me; she just looked up to me so much that she wanted to do everything I did, the way I did it. And all I could do was pulverize her spirit so I could feel better about myself. What an abominable human being I was.

After I finished college, I began planning a move to California, which I completed in October 2005. When the time came for me to leave, I convinced my sister that she should make the cross-country drive with my friend and me. I was elated that she agreed to come. She held my hand from the back seat as I sobbed from homesickness all the way through the Nashville rains. She laughed hysterically with me as we mocked the gaudiness of Graceland near Memphis, and she cried with me when our car was positioned smack-dab between two tornadoes a mile apart on each side as we toured Tornado Alley in Texas. She was my little piece of comfort in the City of Angels, which was so new and different from what we knew growing up.

She stayed with me for almost a week after we got here, and when the time came for her to fly back to Philadelphia, I thought my heart was broken beyond repair. Imagine my rejoicing when, seven months later, she too made the move to Los Angeles, where we both still reside.

Our regular weekend excursions are the glue that holds me together in a state where I have no other blood relatives. She mends my homesickness and restores my sense of humor. We can have an entire conversation consisting only of a fixed gaze at each other from across the room. And I'd be lost without her.

Recipe for love

By Mary Scott

I was a picky eater as a child. Most children are, to some extent, but I really had quirky ideas about food.

For example, I loved corn on the cob. But take it off the cob, cream it, bake it in bread, there was no way I was going to eat it.

Therefore, as you can probably guess, my menu was limited and there wasn't much my mama could do about it. Lucky for me, my pediatrician, Dr. Carter, advised my mother not to force me into eating anything I didn't want to.

However, when my family and I sat down at the supper table and Mama put a kettle of chicken and dumplings in front of me — oh my! — there wasn't much she could do to stop me from eating two, three, even four servings. I'd even scrape the pot with my fingers to get the last bit.

The tender-cooked morsels of chicken paired with her homemade buttermilk dumplings were the stuff of my childhood dreams. For a finicky kid, life just didn't get any better than that.

Even today, Mama's chicken and dumplings taste so good, folks on both the Kentucky and West Virginia sides of the Tug River Valley know about them. When friends hear she's making chicken and dumplings, no fibbin', they come to the door with an empty bowl.

"What do you want?" she'll say to the wayward neighbor.

"I heard you were making chicken and dumplings. I came to see if I could get some."

My childhood was shattered at the age of 14, when my parents divorced. My mama and I, the youngest of six children, moved out of my father's house and into a cramped, little trailer. With her working day and night to support us, she and I rarely spent time together. And she certainly didn't have time to stand over the stove cooking all day.

When she met and married my stepfather, he moved us to Ohio. I hated my new life. I didn't think much of my stepfather, either; but I reckon he felt the same about me.

I had absolutely no friends at my new high school.

I was made to feel stupid by classmates *and* teachers.

My French teacher once remarked that folks from the Appalachian Mountains were ignorant. Then she looked at me and in front of the class said, "You would know about that."

In tears, I begged my mother to let me go back home to Kentucky. She agreed to let me go. I didn't realize then that I would never see her every day ever again.

It was early in the morning when she put me on the Greyhound bus. Looking out the window, into the darkness, I watched as she stood there, alone, crying as the bus pulled away. She was so sad, and I couldn't comfort her.

When I arrived in my hometown, my father was waiting for me. I had hoped to move in with one of my brothers because I didn't want to stay with Dad. I don't know why. I was a mama's girl and maybe I blamed him for their divorce.

Living together was awkward. He tried, but I was cold toward him. We fell into a pattern where I did what I wanted and he didn't say anything about it. I wasn't being bad. I just liked staying away from home, even if that meant staying out all night.

He died of lung cancer a few years later. The last time we saw each other, he let me drive part of the way back to my college in Richmond, Kentucky, and we argued over a traffic light.

I spent two months trying to come to terms with his death. I attempted to cut my wrists with broken glass to put a stop to the never-ending feelings of remorse and guilt. When that didn't work, I left school and home in shame.

I tried to find peace thousands of miles away. What I learned is that no matter how far I went, all that had happened in my life up to that point came with me.

It took years, after living in Hawaii and California, for me to make peace with the bad memories. I missed my dad, and I really missed my mama.

I grew homesick, and eventually began visiting. Fortunately, Mama left that wretched man she married and moved back home.

Whenever I would visit, she would put on a big kettle of

my favorite food just for me. (I've tried making chicken and dumplings for myself, and I've tried the kind in the frozen food aisle at local grocery stores. But neither compares.)

As my mama grows older, the time spent making chicken and dumplings gets tougher on her. There were times I'd go back to see her and she was unable to cook.

Understandably, I'd rather have her rest.

A few years ago, around her birthday, which also falls near Mother's Day, Mama called me to say that her doctor wanted to perform a second open-heart surgery on her, despite her slim chance of surviving. I flew home immediately.

I expected to find her in the hospital when I arrived, but I was relieved to find out that the doctor had changed his mind and sent her home.

When Mama hugged me, she whispered in my ear, "I bought all the makings for dumplings. And I'm going to teach you how to make them."

My dumplings, made under her supervision, were to be served for dinner on Mother's Day.

That morning, she and I put a whole fryer chicken in water to slow-cook. It would be hours before the chicken was cooked through and the broth rich enough.

When the meat fell off the bones, we sat the chicken aside. It was time to make the dumplings. Mama pulled out a big plastic container of all-purpose flour and had me sift some into a bowl. She pulled out the salt and poured some in her hand.

"Just a pinch of salt," she said.

"That's a pinch?" I asked. It looked a more like a tiny handful than a pinch. I tried to make a mental picture of the amount that was in her hand for future reference.

She threw it in the flour.

Then, I learned her secret — something she had kept from me all those years. In a large measuring cup, she spooned chicken broth into some buttermilk.

"Oh, you forgot to tell me that," I said, watching her pour the mixture into the flour.

"Wait a second!" I exclaimed. "How much buttermilk did you put in there?"

"Oh, about a cup or so," she replied.

How was I going to remember this later on?

"Don't you measure out the stuff?" I asked.

"I have *never* measured anything in my life," she responded, as if I had just insulted her.

She went on to tell me that her grandmother taught her to cook intuitively. I guess you're just supposed to know.

Probably sensing my frustration, she put her arm around me and said, "I've got 50 years of doing this on you. A little practice and you'll be fine."

As I mixed the dough, I could tell she was getting tired. I pulled a chair close to the kitchen counter and asked her to sit down. But she didn't want to.

She looked at the dough I was mixing and said it was ready to roll out. She pulled from a cupboard a tall, thin glass vase she liked to use as a rolling pin. She laid down some old newspaper on the kitchen table and told me to sift some flour onto it.

"Place a little bit of your dough in the flour," she instructed, and then taught me to knead the dough in the flour, just enough to get it stiff.

"Roll it out as thin as you can," she said. "After you cut out your squares, pick them up with a little bit of the flour on your hands and put them in the pot. That'll give you your gravy."

As I cut the dough, she went into her room to lie down.

I was feeling good about this until my then-15-year-old niece Natasha came over to the house.

"Maw-maw's not making the dumplings?" she asked.

"No. She's teaching me," I told her.

"Do you have her touch?" she asked seriously, sternly.

"The touch," I thought.

It's not the recipe; it's a natural gift. First intuition and now "touch." I'm doomed.

Finally, the dumplings were done and my heart beat faster thinking about my family trying them. They certainly would say something if they were horrible. (Southerners take their comfort foods seriously.)

"Did Mom make the dumplings?" my brother Jim asked.

"Is he serious, or do they taste so very different than hers even though she helped?" I thought to myself. Then I tried some. Mmmm … not bad. They were close.

I wish my mama could be around always to look over my shoulder whenever I need to do things right. Having her coach me through her recipe made me feel like a kid again — before any bad stuff happened.

I don't know how much longer I'll have her, but one chicken, a little bit of flour and buttermilk and just a "pinch" of salt, mixed with a whole lot of love and one special moment, will keep her close to me forever.

Thank heaven for him

By Ashley M. Ratcliff

W hen I think of him, a flood of memories comes to mind and a smile finds itself planted on my face. For starters, he's a sharply dressed, genuine, big-hearted person with a dynamic sense of humor, an uncanny way with words and an all-around illustrious personality. These attributes, of course, outshine his lesser qualities, such as his affinity for yelling at the television during sporting events, his selective hearing and his penny-pinching tendencies.

That man I just described is my dad, and he's my world. He's a hero in the traditional, American sense of the word: a loving father, dedicated husband and family man, as well as a proud former Marine.

Heavily influenced by my father's profession, my childhood was different from the average kid's. Growing up, my younger brother, Robert Jr., and I ate MREs (meals ready to eat) "just because," learned the importance of a crisp, creased uniform, sang cadence around the house and lived "on base" with all the other "military brats."

One of my fondest memories is eagerly awaiting Dad's arrival home from work to help him remove his tightly laced boots.

With a dad in the armed forces, I had a lot to be proud of, but nothing warms my heart with pride like knowing my dad served in the Gulf War during Operation Desert Storm.

I now realize that it was a tremendous sacrifice.

There's never a good time to go to war, but the timing of my dad's call to duty couldn't have been any worse. My parents had just divorced and they had determined that Dad would have primary custody of us. We were getting settled in our new digs in Irvine, California, when my plans for a pink, princess canopy bed and my brother's dreams of a Power Wheel were put on hold. Our world was turned upside down.

We moved to Detroit, Michigan, with my dad's parents, Grandma Clara and Granddad Freddie, when he was deployed to Saudi Arabia. That was on Aug. 20, 1990, but we were too young (I had just turned 6 and Robert was 5) to understand the gravity of the situation. All we knew was that some bad guy named Saddam Hussein was the reason our pops, then 30 years old, had to leave us.

It's a difficult thing for a youngster to process. To put things into perspective, ever since I can remember, I've been a daddy's girl, literally clinging to my dad every chance I had. I just couldn't let him out of my sight.

When I knew he was about to leave to run an errand or see a friend, I would latch onto his ankles and commence crying my eyes out. Given my fits, my dad's twin sister, Aunt Betty, was in charge of distracting me with the promise of crayons or a new hairdo. There is photographic evidence of me looking like a distraught baby koala wrapped snugly around her papa bear's leg.

So imagine the pain of going from practically spending every hour with your father to suddenly not seeing him at all.

Operation Desert Storm wasn't the first time Dad was away for an extended period — it was the first absence, however, that I can recall. He had spent quite some time on a tour of duty in Okinawa, Japan, when we were tots. My mom would take pictures of my brother and me to send to him, and I would mimic Dad saluting — only my version of the gesture meant touching my index finger to the corner of my right eyebrow.

Dad never wanted us to worry about him while he was in Saudi Arabia. He just trusted that my grandparents, aunts, uncles and cousins would provide us with the care and support that he couldn't give us from the other side of the globe.

My grandparents would watch the news in search of the latest details from the war, and one night I saw my dad's picture on a local TV channel when its anchors honored the servicemen and women in the Middle East. That gave me something to brag about on the schoolyard for the next several weeks.

Dad sent gifts to let us know he was thinking about us and that he was out of harm's way. That Christmas, we received our very first boom box, fully equipped with two tape decks and two microphones. It kept us busy, even if we annoyed our family members in the process. Finding creative ways to express ourselves and being around lots of relatives no doubt soothed the sting of missing our father.

Dad tried his best to keep sane — he worked out, read the Bible, prayed, watched movies and wrote letters. He never shared with us how terrifying his wartime experience really was. Whenever we asked, he would just say that Saudi was extremely hot or he would talk about the language barrier. He even brought back Pepsi cans written in Arabic script.

Now that I'm old enough to know the truth, I recently had a conversation with my father to bring some closure to the questions that kept me up at night.

My dad worked in telecommunications, so he wasn't on the front lines. He said he was about 25 miles from "the action" but still found himself in some pretty hairy situations.

There was the time when Hussein set the oil fields on fire, creating the impression that the sky was gone. Dad and his comrades were in total darkness for about a week — no sun at all. Another time, the Iraqi dictator's minions fired Scud missiles, forcing the U.S. soldiers into bunkers, uncertain where the projectiles would land.

After what seemed like ages, Dad returned to the States on March 22, 1991. My brother and I were so thankful that God sent our daddy home safely, and he picked up right where he left off, showering us with love.

I brought Dad to my first-grade class for show-and-tell, and reveled in the fact that my classmates and teacher treated him like a celebrity. All the while I clung to him like I used to, afraid to let go. He was all mine from then on.

My dad retired in 2004 after 20 years of service in the U.S. Marine Corps. He is proof that the saying "once a Marine, always a Marine" holds true. I enjoy the moments when he regales any and all who will listen with candid stories about his career, especially his stint as a drill instructor.

Dad said he was able to provide for his family a lot better by joining the Marines than if we had stayed back in Detroit, where I was born.

All these years later, I still find myself proud of my dad. He continues to better himself, whether it is through attending church and applying what he's learned there in his daily walk, or completing a rigorous, prestigious leadership program for his civilian job and working on earning a degree.

It's a privilege to have such a strong relationship with my father. We're both Cancers, both sensitive souls. We have confided in each other during tender, trying moments.

It's a blessing that my father always has been an active participant in my upbringing.

It was Dad who took me shopping for my first training bra and bought me my first diary.

It was Dad who taught me how to ride a bike and gave me the "birds and bees" talk.

It was Dad who encouraged me to pick up the violin and supported my girlhood career ambition of becoming an artist.

It was Dad who helped move me into my first apartment and offered me sage advice during my first real heartbreak.

Yes, he was strict and had high expectations, and there were many times — especially during my teen years — when we didn't see eye to eye. But I am glad we overcame the obstacles together.

Thank heaven for my father and the precious bond we share.

A whirlwind first crush

By Rebecca Villaneda

You never forget your first love — even if he's on stage 50 feet away from you, or on TV dancing and singing like the superstar that he is.

Try finding a notebook from my adolescent years where the name Jordan Knight isn't scrawled across it. It won't happen.

If, from the age 12 through 16, my job was collecting magazines, buttons, lunch boxes, T-shirts, blankets or puzzles with his mug and the rest of the New Kids on the Block on it, recording TV appearances, or buying at least two copies of every album (one to play, one to keep pristine), I would be a rich little girl.

I remember the first time I heard their music. It was at the swap meet in Torrance, California, in 1989, when I was in about sixth grade. My mom bought me "Hangin' Tough" on cassette, and I played it on my pink boom box again and again.

Looking at the photo on the 2.5-inch-by-4-inch cover, I thought right away Joe McIntyre was going to be my favorite.

But after magazines were purchased and the group was in the spotlight more and more, it was clear Jordan Knight was the one who was going to inundate my mind for years to come.

His voice, his dreamy face, his charming, shy demeanor, and endless talent hypnotized me and kept my mind full of fantasies and visions of bliss.

But there were four others to complete the group that I would love for a lifetime: Danny Wood's muscles and awesome smile; Joe's blue eyes and humor; Jon Knight's quietness and authentic, genuine heart; and Donnie Wahlberg's love and belief in us, the fans, and his all-around bitchin' personality that makes you feel like you're the only one in the room.

It wouldn't make sense minus one of them. Ever.

Their combination, their personalities have been permanently etched in my heart and mind.

I sit here trying to explain why I, plus thousands of other women, feel this way about five men, and it's hard. When it's a gut feeling, when it affects you inside, how do you put that into words? They just affect you. Their smiles, their voices, and their mannerisms, even their hands — I can recognize them all right away. I wish I could explain it better. Or maybe I don't want to, because the emotions, the unconditional love I have for them, are mine.

They are the reason I love music so much. Their eclectic styles and tastes made me want to search for what they were into and what they were listening to. They have made, and continue to make, an impression on me.

There's a special connection those five men made with millions of women across the world that nobody — well, perhaps a Beatles' fan — can explain or understand. I'm not comparing the New Kids to The Beatles; I'm comparing the electric, lustful and magnetic connection we fans have to them.

Posters lined my walls, sometimes in plastic sheets, so as not to ruin their crisp, clean edges. It was everything New Kids, all the time, everywhere.

The phenomenon that is the New Kids on the Block is a part of me, and those around me accepted it as part of who I am. My best friend at the time, Susan, and I would write stories about them and us — tales that filled about 10 notebooks. I recorded every single show they ever made an appearance on. If the VHS didn't work, I'd set up my video camera on a chair, on top of the right amount of books, and record the TV.

Comic books, coloring books, their cartoons, their dolls and toy stage, I had to have it all.

Theirs was my first official concert in 1990 — the Magic Summer Tour at Dodger Stadium in Los Angeles. It was all very surreal, and thoughts of "I'm breathing the same air as they are!" crossed my mind. I had to ditch the sign I made, and when the gal collecting it said the New Kids would see it later on, I actually wrote my home phone number on it. I was only 12 and they were well into their 20s, but it didn't matter.

I even made my own New Kids on the Block fan club with

the neighborhood girls and handmade our club cards. The New Kids brought out my creativity on many levels. I was making video montages of my favorite New Kids' moments — and this was before computers.

Going into high school, the dedication continued. Somehow during my junior and senior years I convinced friends — female and male — to perform to New Kids songs at our talent shows.

But let's rewind to my sophomore year, when I was, let's say, braver. I formed a crew that was going to finally lead me to meet them.

There was a new album, "Face the Music," and a new tour, but on a much smaller scale. Susan and I went to an autograph signing in the City of Industry. But we got there late and they cut off the line. However, as Jordan and Joe, the only two New Kids there, came out of the club, I screamed Jordan's name. I didn't get any reaction.

He got into the limo, but I wasn't done. I walked to the other side of the limo and opened the door. It was unlocked. There he was, 2 feet away from me. Both of us froze, shocked at what just happened, and we each waited for the other to make a move. But the limo driver interjected. Damn limo driver.

Strike one.

Fast-forward a month or two, to April 1994. I made my brother take me and three other 15-year-olds to the Ventura Theatre in Ventura, California, at about 10 p.m. the night before their show, which was only my second New Kids on the Block concert. We spent the night outside the theater with blankets we planned to ditch. We made friends with some young women and actually got a ride back to L.A. with them. We had tickets to the show there a day later.

Their buses arrived. I went crazy — as did the hundreds of girls around me. I clearly remember Danny's satisfied nod and grin as he looked at all of us screaming girls.

Then Jordan — the love of my life — came out and I rushed him, but a huge arm pushed me away before I could get to him. Damn bodyguard.

Strike two.

We missed school the next day and took a taxi to Hollywood. We staked out the then-Bel Age Hotel on Sunset Boulevard because we knew they were making an appearance on "The Arsenio Hall Show" the afternoon prior to their concert.

There he was, a tired Jordan, walking to the van from the lobby. I couldn't contain myself; I ran toward him. But another bodyguard got to me first. Damn, another bodyguard.

Strike three.

My perfect Jordan moment, again, was interrupted. I still had faith.

Then the unthinkable happened. Rumors of their breakup came true. Jon's absence from this last tour made it suspect that the end was near; and then they canceled the rest of the tour. It was true and I was sad, but deep down I felt that it wasn't over. There was more to be said, more that they needed to prove, that this wasn't a fad.

The summer of 1994 — the year they broke up — I spent a month in Europe. I was on a mission to buy hard-to-find memorabilia, and I did. That winter, I went to Boston with my sister and her now-husband, and I made them drive me to Jamaica Plains to find what I still think was Joe's childhood home. I found NKOTB's star at the Tower Records in Boston and asked a stranger on the street to take my picture as I hugged the floor around the plaque.

Movies starring Donnie, and TV shows and solo albums featuring Joe, Jordan and Danny kept me content the years in between as I waited to get my perfect Jordan moment.

I met all but Jon during those years; I met Donnie and Danny at one of Joe's shows.

In the meantime, I did, however, meet Kelly, the girl who was to become my New Kids on the Block partner in crime — the girl who was going to go with me on my future NKOTB adventures. I met her at the premiere of Donnie's very first starring-role movie, "Southie," in 1998 in Culver City, California.

I ran into her again at a Jordan meet-and-greet at the KIIS FM radio studio near Burbank. I got a quick picture with Jordan, no interruptions this time, but it was far from perfect. I also was able to attend a preshow meet-and-greet with him at one of his solo concerts at the House of Blues in Anaheim — still far from perfect.

Then, I got the best gift — a second chance to re-live my schoolgirl crush.

And yes, it was amazing to get pictures with them, but it never felt right because it was with them individually. I fell in love with them as a package.

The rumors of a reunion started in 2008, when www.nkotb. com displayed a new home page with a "stay tuned" message.

Kelly and I didn't know what to expect, but we knew we were game for whatever they were planning. A new album was confirmed through an appearance on the "Today Show" in New York in April 2008. I woke up early and stared at the TV, waiting for their five-minute appearance announcing that they were getting back together — all five of them. My heart raced and I squealed like I had in the past, excited that my youth was being rejuvenated.

It's like anything is possible when they are in the equation.

No obstacles exist and all things stand still while I am with them or simply enjoying the thought of them.

It's a little like magic. Inhibitions are lost, fantasy sets in, and I just want to live to see what is next. They bring me back to an innocence I cherish and a feeling that makes me want to take chances, let loose and be free.

What girl doesn't need an escape now and then? They initiate my daydreams and then make them tangible.

The New Kids have indeed re-banded in the last two years, and now I'm equipped with a passport, my own money, the will, an invitation and a Joe girl (Kelly) by my side. We've had amazing adventures chasing our five favorite Boston boys.

Still, after all these years, I feel nostalgic for a time when life wasn't so difficult — when my weekend plans consisted of getting a NKOTB dance routine down and setting up my camera to record myself performing it.

I was lucky enough to be one of a handful of fans to see their first performance in front of a crowd in 15 years at the House of Blues on Sunset Boulevard in May 2008. It was a rehearsal show that was just days before their first live, televised performance on the "Today Show" on May 16, 2008. Yes, I went to that as well.

You see? They make me live. They make me say, "To hell with everything else; you only live once."

New Kids on the Block held an autograph signing after the performance at the Macy's in NYC. There they all were, lined up in front of me, waiting to meet and greet me and about 200 others who endured the rainy morning. I realize now, this was my perfect Jordan moment — meeting and talking with him and the rest of the New Kids all at once. Something I never, in nearly 20 years of admiration, got to experience. It was a special moment for me. I remember stepping back and inhaling it for all it was.

Concerts in Boston, Las Vegas, Concord, Santa Barbara and L.A., with preshow meet-and-greets, will never get old.

And then the unimaginable happened — in May 2009, one year after their reunion, the New Kids organized a cruise from Miami to the Bahamas for about 1,500 lucky fans. Of course, Kelly and I were onboard. And we went on their second weekend cruise in May 2010.

If not now, when? That's my motto. And feeling like a carefree teenager is the power behind my uninhibited, opportunistic moves that get me in front of a New Kid. I wouldn't be me without them.

Part II:
Growing

Full circle

By Rebecca Villaneda

June 5, 1998.

You never forget the day you lose your mom — the woman who is the most important force in your life.

It happened four days before my 20th birthday — unfair.

Her name was Anna Maria DeHaro Villaneda.

She wore cute, A-line dresses with collars, accessorized by gloves and kitten heels.

She was popular.

I knew she was battling cancer, but my immature 19-year-old mind couldn't comprehend anything further than what was happening socially around me.

I had just moved out with my best friend, Shelly, to the Hollywood area. We thought we had it made: living by our own rules, having boys over, and having fake IDs that easily allowed us to enter the Roxy, the Viper Room, and the Whiskey A Go Go.

That's what my life was about at the time.

Life was sweet. But it was soon interrupted one night while we were playing cards at our place. I got a phone call from my brother — the person in our family who knew best how to talk to me.

He asked me to take the phone call away from everyone, and to listen to him carefully.

I can't remember the entire conversation. Just a few words … "Mom is very sick. We have to be strong and prepared."

It didn't sink in then; it didn't sink in months later. Still, to this day — 11 years after her passing — it's hard to realize she is no longer with me.

I still was sitting pretty at my apartment when hospice moved into the family home. A hospital bed was placed at the end of my parents' king-size bed and that's where Mom was to spend the rest of her days.

For a person who attracted light and people, and was a genuinely giving and loving person, it was painful to see her weaken.

It also was hard to see Dad dwindle with her. His hair and mustache turned extra gray and he lost weight along with her. He took some verbal abuse from her, but he took it like a soldier.

Mom's best friend and brother, my *Tío* Sam, came to visit from Mexico, and he helped shave her head. It was appropriate that he did that because they were extremely close and had a relationship like no other. They got along so nicely and laughed most of the time they were together. They had an unspoken bond that everyone respected.

The day my *Tia* Rosita, one of my mom's older sisters, came to visit, she cried at the first sight of what my mom had become: a fragile and noncommunicative cancer patient — the complete opposite of what she was as a youngster.

Back in the small town where Mom grew up, Jerez, Zacatecas — a city north of Guadalajara, Mexico — she was the first female to learn how to drive a U-Haul-type truck. Her parents owned a small market, so she and my grandfather would get produce from the ranches and bring it into town. Those two, I hear, were very close. I never met my grandfather, but according to the stories, he was a legend in the town. I was told that he killed his mistress' husband; he fought with the infamous Pancho Villa at *La Bufa* in Zacatecas, and received medals for his valiant efforts. His medals hang in my cousin Rutita's home in Susticacan, Mexico. Rutita's mother, my *Tia* Elvira, recently celebrated her 90th birthday.

My family has strong roots in Mexico, and it's a goal of mine to write our history, if anything, in honor of Mom.

The days leading up to her death were painful, frustrating and tiresome for the whole family.

Besides my dad, I have three siblings: my brother, Frankie, and my two sisters, Liz and Ruthie. They all are older than me by at least nine years.

Each of us dealt with Mom's death in our own way, and selfishly, we all thought about the milestones in our lives that

she would miss — weddings, grandchildren, college graduations, et cetera.

In actuality, I lost my mom months prior to her passing. As the tumor in her head grew, it took her personality away, which, in a way, prepared us for the day that we would no longer physically see her.

Her mobility almost was gone and her speech hardly made sense.

She wore a diaper and her life came full circle, as did our relationship. I cared for her innocent life as she did mine when I was a child. I helped change her diaper as she did mine during my baby years.

One conversation stands out like a thorn in my side. I can hear it play out in my head like it was just yesterday.

I can't remember how it came up but, knowing my mom, she had been planning it, or at least made some time for just her and me to sit together.

She said, "You know I'm always going to be taking care of you … even if it's from heaven."

We both cried because it was unfair and painfully true.

She had accepted that her illness was winning and she, as a mother, was trying to prepare me for it.

Similarly, my sister Ruthie climbed into bed with her. They both were lying on their sides, and while Ruthie was trying to comfort her, my mom found the strength in her feeble body to squeeze Ruthie's hand, to gesture that everything was going to be OK.

The morning she died — June 5, 1998 — we all were home, sleeping around Mom on my parents' bed and on the floor, and my brother-in-law, Harry, was in the living room.

We were given fair warning, thanks to the hospice binder details. They really map out for you what to expect when someone is nearing death.

The noises she was making, insensitively called "the death rattle," were driving me crazy. She looked like she was sleeping.

I went to my room — I can't remember what I was thinking. I was probably just scared, confused, and I couldn't handle the noise or seeing her like that anymore. I was mad, I was sad, and

I thought God was being cruel. I think I cursed at Him on more than one occasion.

My brother came to get me. He shook me on the shoulder. I can't remember exactly what he said, but it was something like, "I think it's time. I think she's gone."

Robotically, I got up. And as I walked back to my family, it was like God and my brother were holding my hands. I walked in and everyone was sobbing around her.

My poor dad. I hate seeing him cry.

She was gone. She was there physically, but no longer was she breathing.

It happened at about 2 a.m.

I learned afterward that, while I was in my bedroom, Liz and Frankie held her and talked with her, and Frankie gave her the blessing to let go. Minutes after, she did.

She breathed her last breath.

I realized recently that I haven't thought about my mom or her persona as much. In my life, she's become my angel, but it made me sad that I hadn't thought about her lovely laugh, her swallowing hug, her thoughtfulness, her vibrant smile and radiant aura. Those all are still as clear as day, and I hope to make it a point to think about them more often.

I also remember how much she loved to write letters to people. I can see her script handwriting now, on lined paper or inside one of her many cards she had waiting to send to the right person.

She was a special lady, and someone who still comes up in my family's daily conversations.

She was my No.-1 fan, and no one can ever live up to that role in my life. I just hope I can one day be someone's biggest fan like she was mine.

As a kid, her love made me feel like anything was possible, and she encouraged my creativity. She fed it, in fact.

When she died, a piece of me left with her.

I knew I would never fear death from that point on, not because I will get to be with her again, but because when you lose the one person who understands you, who will always let you be who you want to be and love you unconditionally, nothing is scary.

Nothing can ever be that hard.

Having to say goodbye to my mom was the most difficult thing I ever have gone through or will ever endure.

You never get over it. You never make sense of it, but you learn to make peace with it.

That morning, as the sun began to rise, we sat around her and prayed while Dad poured holy water on her palms.

I was mad, exhausted and hurt that she left me, but relieved that she wasn't in pain anymore.

Her funeral service, for us, was a way to celebrate her life. We made a video montage of photos and even black-and-white snapshots of my parents' honeymoon.

It's still hard for me to watch that video and I haven't for years, but I'm so grateful my sisters put it together.

Mariachis played at the house following her church service, and people stayed late, reminding me of how many lives Mom touched.

While she was ill, Mom decided to be cremated, and so she was. We have her remains in an urn on the mantel, surrounded by two pictures of her — one in her youth and one of her older.

Dad makes a point to put fresh flowers next to her, and I've even invited my nieces and nephews to do so on occasion.

They never met Mom, but the oldest, Anna, bears her name.

I feel her presence around me and know that her promise to watch over me holds true.

My own

By Amy Higgins Artino

We finally arrived in Los Angeles on Oct. 5, 2005, after nearly a week on the road. We saw Nashville in the rain, Texas just before the floods came and Tombstone in the blistering, dry heat. I can't wait to go back there. All the streets and most of the buildings are originals, and I can almost smell the horses and cowboys, and the booze on Wyatt Earp's breath. It's incredible. I honestly must have lived a past life in the 1800s Wild West, as I felt such a sense of belonging — it's one I have never felt anywhere else but at home.

Arizona's Dragoon Mountains were spectacular! Until this trip, I had never seen mountains so huge in my life. Everything I thought I knew as a mountain now is merely a hill in my mind. The way the sunset was painted around the mountaintops simply is indescribable — the mountains, merely giant shadows against the blushing backdrop, seem to stand sentinel over the entire landscape. Even the state's Painted Desert pales in comparison. While I'm awestruck and in love with everything I have seen on the way, it really drives home how far away I am.

I can't believe how much I miss Pennsylvania and my family. I feel so removed from everyone here, but I love being in the land of eternal sunshine — and in his bed every night. It's comforting to know we will wake up each morning and go to sleep each night beside each other now, in the same room, instead of just underneath the same sky. He feels like a little piece of home in an otherwise foreign place.

I thought the trip out to California would be the adventure, but I realize the adventure is just beginning now that I'm here. I guess my first order of business is to find a job. It's so strange being away from the familiar, not under Mom and Dad's roof, on my own for the first time. The laundry piles up. The bathroom stays dirty until I clean it. The meals go uncooked, unserved, uneaten unless I initiate the tasks. I have to seek out the smiles and greetings that I am used to getting from my mother when I walk in the door. I have to call my dad on the phone if I want his input, his advice — to say goodnight. It's terrifying.

Sometimes the fear and uncertainty threaten to choke me to death in my sleep. Sometimes the tears and the pain and longing, the weight of homesickness feel like they may crush me, suffocate me, bury me alive. But I *need* to be here; it's this innate "knowing" of that fact, but for what, how long and why, I don't know. It makes it hard for others to understand my need to up and leave home to be here, with no plan, no concrete idea of where I'm headed or what I plan to do. And no one is more frustrated by this than I am. Do they think this is *easy*?! All they see is me, running away from the safe, the concrete, the familiar, to be with him, but you can't help who you love or what you need to do to keep it. Or control whatever it is your destiny sometimes has to drag you, kicking and screaming, to do.

And besides, he is only a scrap of the equation. He isn't the only thing keeping me here. He isn't even the only thing that brought me here. Still, at least there is no more distance, no more longing, no more need to worry that someone else will satisfy his needs. No concern of "out of sight, out of mind." I am here. He is here. It's all that matters. We will overcome. We will prevail. I am his and he is mine.

It's done. He broke it off. I'm here in this crazy, faraway place, and now I'm completely alone. I came all this way to make it easier on him, on me, on us, and now, just weeks into this venture, he thinks he can do better than me? I challenge him to try. And I have nowhere to go to escape but the living room. This apartment — *his* apartment — is my new home, and I have no money to get my own place because I've only just begun my new job. The tense energy between us as we sleep back to back — neither of us wants the discomfort of the couch — is stifling. I keep praying he will roll over and change his mind, look at me sleeping and want to take it all back. Tell me he is sorry and start over. Love me, feel me, make me his again. But he won't. He just keeps snoring, unconsciously inching away. He's a zombie in the morning, and the strain is unbearable. I am broken. I am so lonely. And I love him, and can't understand how he thinks he could find a better mate than the one who all but walked 3,000 miles to be with him. But he has a need. And I have to just sit back and watch, and get dressed and undressed away from his eyes, as if we are strangers who just met for the first time. There is shyness, a formal air that should not be. And I hate it. This person with whom I've swapped tears, memories, fears, laughter, kisses, dreams, and life is now as known to me as an alien. Who is this guy? What are his hopes, his fears, his dreams? What makes him tick? It's as if when he said, "I think we should see other people," I was given amnesia of all this person is. His face is so familiar, his scent, his breath on my face and yet — I know him not at all. I have to grieve on the walks to and from the gym, in my car, in the bathroom at work — anywhere and everywhere away from his eyes, because once I get back to the apartment at the end of the day, the charade begins: How happy I am in this new place, how fulfilling and promising this new job is, and how much I'm enjoying this newfound freedom as a single woman in L.A. How much I don't miss him and agree that this break is exactly what we need. How totally and completely OK I am without him. On my own. My own.

When I woke up this morning, I looked in the mirror and, for the first time, I saw a girl I did not recognize staring back at me. For the first time, I am not my father's. I am not my mother's. I am not his. I am my own.

And don't call me 'Girly'

By Mary Scott

Had one of my four brothers called me "Girly" or "Girly Girl," I would have assumed it was yet another attempt at sibling annoyance. Coming from a sea-salt-crusted old man — one who spent the entire movement for women's rights aboard a U.S. Navy aircraft carrier — "Girly" was just a downright, plain ol' insult. It was just one way of putting me in my place.

Being a woman in the military is tough duty. I recently heard an ex-Army veteran say, "Being a woman in the military is like being in war all the time."

It's a man's world, and don't let anyone ever tell you differently. Even today, when women have more access to opportunity, there are men who believe there is no place in the military for women.

When I joined in 1985 at age 20, I had just dropped out of college and had no idea of what to do.

I came from a Navy family, so the idea of enlisting came to mind. My father, Charles, served aboard a submarine chaser in the Pacific during World War II. My oldest brother, Chuck, was a Navy radioman during the Vietnam War. Another brother, Sam, was a Navy Seabee in the late 1970s. My brothers Jim and John, however, did not follow family tradition. Jim went into the Army, like his idol, Elvis Presley, and John remained a civilian.

My biggest influence for joining the Navy was my sister, Sue. She was one of the few female electronic technicians when she joined in the early '70s.

I admired Sue for leaving home when she did. Women in my hometown were expected to marry a coal miner and push out a litter of children. But Sue defied expectations and became an independent woman.

When I found myself penniless after less than two years of college, I thought the way toward my own independence was through the military.

On the surface, my service seemed perfect. I went to boot camp in Orlando, Florida, served active duty at the Naval Air Station Barbers Point, Hawaii, and did reserve time in Point Loma, San Diego. Harsh, eh?

I had great choices of locations, for sure. But every day was a battle for respect.

If someone wasn't grabbing your ass, others were making you do all the work or keeping you from it, or trying to alienate

you. Women had to work harder and better just to prove they could do the job.

Harassment, sexual and otherwise, was, and is, prominent in military life for women.

In the mid-'80s, most of the older men I served with had

been out at sea for much of their careers. NAS Barbers Point was the first shore duty for many of them. At that time, there were few ships women could serve aboard, so women filled the jobs on land bases, forcing the guys out to sea. This caused a lot of resentment, and some of the men often took it out on us.

And, of course, for many of the older men, they felt the women should drop their weapons and pick up aprons.

I often was told to make the coffee. I didn't drink it at the time. (Funny, today I can't live without it.)

More than once, I'd hear some chief say, "Hey, Girly, why don't you make some coffee?"

I'd answer their question with a question: "Why should I make it?"

The response: "Because you're a girl. And girls make the coffee."

The women, we all complied; we had to. After all, it was against military code to disobey an order from a superior.

But I hated it. And I especially hated to be called "Girly," or worse yet, "Girly Girl." I was a young woman — not a girl, and definitely not girly — serving my country. I deserved more respect than that.

Once when I was told to make the coffee, I thought about my mama and a story she told me once. My mama's philosophy is to "get mad, *then* get even."

When she was younger, Mama was helping her Aunt Sis serve a family dinner. Her Uncle Jim ordered her to pour him a cup of coffee. (He was a disrespectful bastard in many other ways, too.)

Having endured enough of him, Mama got the coffeepot, walked to the dining table and stood next to him.

"Say when," she told him as she began to pour the coffee into his cup.

"That's enough," he said.

But she kept pouring.

"I said that's enough!"

She kept pouring, and the coffee started to overflow.

He jumped up and yelled, "I told you to stop! What's wrong with you?"

"I told you to say, 'When.'"

He never ordered her to pour him a cup of coffee from that time on.

I figured if that worked for her, perhaps something similar would work for me.

Hmmm ...

As I stood over the large, catering-style coffee maker, scooping the coffee grinds from the canister into the pot, the words "keep pouring" repeated in my head.

So I did. I poured in scoop after scoop after scoop after scoop. I made that coffee so strong, so dark, and *so* thick, I could have used it to paint my barracks room.

As the chiefs and first-class petty officers entered the office and one by one placed their cups under the spout, I watched with the utmost interest. The coffee drizzled into their cups like molasses.

And, one by one, they spat it out.

"Who made this crap?" asked one chief.

"I did. Don't you like it?" I said pridefully.

"No, it tastes like motor oil."

"Well, I don't drink coffee, so I never know how much to put in the pot."

"Do us a favor, Scotty, and don't make the coffee anymore."

"Aw. Are you sure? I *enjoy* making it so much."

"I'm sure."

"OK. If that's what you want."

Only one seriously flawed chief liked it. I think that's because he actually did drink motor oil.

I left the head office to drive out to my regular workshop with one of the biggest smiles on my face. I won!

After that, I never had to make coffee again. One of the "boys" in my duty section took my place doing that chore.

I know it was a small thing, but I cherish what I did on that day. *That* was the day I learned how to fight back.

It's strictly platonic

By Ashley M. Ratcliff

Whoever said men and women can't be "just friends" is a bold-faced liar. You see, my best friend (the male version), Ronilo, and I are living proof that a boy and a girl can share the joys of friendship without romantic feelings getting in the way.

Of course, I have a female best friend, Yvette, who is my heart. But I also am blessed with a right-hand man who knows me just as well. And what an unlikely duo we make. He's a Filipino boy who surfs, makes his own juices, reads inspirational books, and socializes with celebrities for work. I'm an African-American girl who prefers a warm night inside, feasts on fast food, indulges in reality television shows, and has made a career of interviewing local heroes.

I've known Ronilo since the fifth grade, when I moved to

San Diego. We didn't start off as two peas in a pod like we are now, either. He was interested in chasing the girls around the playground and hanging out with his older sister's cool friends. I, on the other hand, latched onto a group of girls who made me — the shy, new girl — feel welcomed. As the years passed, our circle of friends became intertwined — in part because that little heartbreaker dated many of my girlfriends. He and his family moved away during middle school to the desert town of Ridgecrest, California. Life moved on.

It wasn't until much later that our bond evolved into what it is today, as we both saw ourselves in the same situation: away at college — he at Brooks Institute of Photography in Ventura and I just up the coast at the University of California, Santa Barbara.

He was the human equivalent of comfort food, that familiar face I could trust among a sea of strangers with unknown pasts and intentions. I was that for him, too, but also somewhat of a personal therapist when he experienced an intense breakup with a mutual friend of ours. That's when we really got to know each other. The phone calls at all hours of the day, the long drives back down to San Diego, even the arguments about trivial, mundane things are the foundation that established this friendship.

As with my female friends, I can discuss or do anything and everything with Ronilo. But there are times when he and I will be out and about doing things that best friends do — shopping, going to the movies, having dinner, et cetera — and passersby make the assumption that we're an item. I can't tell you how

many stares, whispers and glances we've received. It's gotten to the point where we brush it off and, in unison, say, "Yes, we're an interracial couple." We've even joked about placing this slogan on matching T-shirts for all to see.

There's an unmistakable "friendship line" rid of any hint of sexual tension. We've never crossed it and have no desire to take it there. It's simple, really. We have a clearly defined, strictly platonic relationship. It's just others who don't get it.

And that, unfortunately, sometimes causes strife: jealous girlfriends and insecure boyfriends, namely. I get the subtle but spiteful: "Wow, you guys are so in sync." He gets the curiously cynical: "Are you sure you've never dated?"

It doesn't help, though, that he gets a kick out of introducing his highly traditional family members to me as his fiancée. It's the shock value or the anticipated reaction that gives him a juvenile sense of excitement. Meanwhile, all I can do is avert my eyes, shake my head and remark what an idiot he is.

Perhaps others' confusion about "what we are" stems from the comfort level that is apparent from observing us interact. I've been told that I'm a "guy's girl." Maybe that has something to do with it. We say, "I love you" before we get off the phone because we mean it. He's even lived on my futon for months at a time in between finding the right place. We know just about everything about each other — and that comes from years of learning what makes the other tick.

I found out the hard way that Ronilo's a ninny when it comes to spicy foods the time we went to eat Vietnamese phó soup, which happened to be garnished with jalapeño peppers. He turned bright red, began sweating profusely, and demanded water. Never again.

I discovered just how generous he can be from the many times during college that he drove an hour out of his way to pick me up just to hang out, the countless dinners he prepared or purchased for me, and the way he let me become a part of his life.

No matter how full Ronilo is there always is room in his stomach for a strawberry shortcake ice cream bar. He claims to be a stud but really is a chicken when it comes to approaching attractive women. He despises any hint of an "attitude" but feels he's entitled to that latitude in his own delivery. An exceptional command of the English language is not his strong suit, especially when he constantly butchers common phrases, like saying, "Ignorance is a bliss."

Likewise, there are plenty of nuances that he knows about me. All it takes is one look to ignite or extinguish a disagreement. Nine times out of 10, I'm going to need that extra blanket or sweater. A night of karaoke just isn't complete without signing a Journey or *NSYNC tune, and the fun doesn't end until my voice gives out. If I had my way, pizza would be on my dinner plate every night. Taking me on a hike in 85-degree weather at Runyon Canyon while I'm wearing Chuck Taylors is not a good idea. I'm a firm believer that pet goldfish are capable of being loved (rest in peace, Hand Jive). Seeing beyond skin color is a virtue that more people should possess.

Another reason I value our friendship is that Ronilo provides the male perspective I need in my day-to-day situations. I like that I can pick his brain about the opposite sex — often phrased as a question: "What does it mean when a guy says/does (fill in the blank)?" — and get a straight answer.

More than a friend, throughout the years he has become part of my family. He's like a brother to me; he's my protector and caregiver when I'm so far away from my parents and siblings.

I sometimes contemplate how things would be if we hadn't reconnected during college, how my worldview and personality would differ. Much of who I am is due in part to life's little lessons that Ronilo and I have learned together. So, I'd rather not entertain that thought for too long.

Part III:
Worst nightmare

According to the U.S. Department of Justice,
60 percent of sexual assaults go unreported.

Dislodging the demons

I don't remember all the details of it because I've spent the last 10 years or so trying to block them out. I was either 19 or 20; I can't remember which. It was near the end of April, though, because we had tickets to see "Rent" in the city for my birthday — his little way of trying to change my mind about him. I guess it was obvious my heart had cooled over. I wanted to end things, but I didn't know how. Not that he would let me.

What I do remember is that it happened in my dorm room on the eighth floor of the building. I had the top bunk, and my jersey-knit comforter was a dusty-plum color. My roommate was at a night class, so he wanted to take advantage of the "alone time." All I really wanted was some time to myself. He usurped all of it. I told him I felt sick, which was a lie; I really just didn't want to because I wasn't attracted to him anymore, but I was too afraid to tell him so. I didn't know what he would do or say, and he was volatile and unpredictable.

He started to unbutton my jeans, and I pleaded with him to stop. I just didn't have it in me to suffer it again. The truth was, he disgusted me. He proceeded anyway. It was my duty, he told me. I was his, and it was part of the deal. But I begged to differ. What happened to my right to choose? My free will? I was screaming inside, but on the outside, I was silent.

"Is this rape?" I remember thinking.

Then, answering my own question, I insisted it couldn't be. I was his girlfriend. Sex was expected. It wasn't like I could press charges. How could I ever prove I hadn't consented? It would be his word against mine, and he was "in" with public safety on campus, thanks to working nights for them.

It wasn't until years later that I found out anyone can rape you — husbands, parents, boyfriends, and friends. All that mattered was whether or not you consented. How stupid I was.

He tugged at my zipper. I tried to roll away. He was getting increasingly frustrated with me.

"Just come on," he said.

He started getting rougher with me, trying to keep me on my back while he pulled down his pants. I finally relented. It was easier than trying to fight him off. But I hated every last second of it. I didn't even try to fake pleasure. Tears stung my eyes, but I refused to let them fall — it would only encourage him to be more insolent toward me. I was mortified, imagining what my then-recently deceased grandfather would say. He promised he'd watch over me always, and I wanted to die at the thought that this was what he would see. He would be so ashamed of me. I lay there and tried to go elsewhere in my head until he finally finished using my body. It was then I realized that he failed to use protection. When the initial shock wore off, I exploded in anger.

It wasn't because he'd forgotten; I knew it was intentional, though he never assumed I was smart enough to figure that out — he was hoping to get me pregnant so I couldn't leave him, so we'd always be bound by something. He hadn't even considered my feelings, wants, or desires. I mattered not at all. He didn't care that in my head it wasn't being a young, unwed mother that I was afraid of; it's that I refused to let my child have him as a father. That I was hell-bent against being linked to him for life.

I began freaking out, and he pretended to be distraught, like it was all an accident. When I finally regained my senses, I called Planned Parenthood and immediately made an appointment for emergency contraception. The soonest they could see me was the next day. Seeing that I was far from pleased, and always feigning the knight-in-shining-armor bit, he apologized more profusely and said he wanted to go to the clinic with me for support. I hated him.

The next morning, he drove us to the clinic. I processed to the door, ashamed, through the crowd of abortion protesters who could only assume the worst of me. I wanted to die.

He waited with me while I filled out paperwork. I was terrified someone would think he was my husband. When I was called back to the exam room, a sweet, nonjudgmental woman explained the pill to me. She assured me it wasn't an abortion pill, but one that would prevent pregnancy. She said it might make me feel ill, but that Dramamine would help. I was to take one with my next meal and one 12 hours after that. I left with the pills and the instructions, and we went to grab some food. He cried in the parking lot, afraid that "we'd" just made a decision to kill "his" baby. I told him it wasn't an abortion pill. I really hated him.

I took the first pill within the hour, and then I went back to the dorm to nap while he went to class. I awoke about two hours later, finding it was dark outside. I have never felt so sick in my entire life. It was like having the worst case of the stomach flu you can imagine. The Dramamine was a joke; my sickness had nothing to do with equilibrium issues.

I was expected to show up to watch some performance he was supposed to do that night at the Student Union Center, but I could barely walk without nearly fainting or dry heaving. I called to tell him so. He insisted I be there. Being the weak personage he'd turned me into, I went.

I was as sick as a dog all night and was really upset because we were supposed to take a train to the city to see "Rent" in the morning. I wasn't sure I could even stand up. He insisted on spending the night so that he could wake me up to take the second dose of the pill. I just wanted to die.

In the morning, I got up as planned and tried to get dressed for the city. I couldn't move without fainting or throwing up. It was hell. He said he couldn't take me on a train like that — "people would stare." And there I was, feeling guilty. He reminded me how much he had spent on the theater tickets and that it was all going to waste. Since I'd ruined the whole day anyway, he left, slamming the door behind him. I sobbed myself back to sleep.

Summer of pain

Somehow, that summer we were still together. He was attending a police academy program in a nearby beach community. I went down to visit him one day, and that's when it all got much worse. Having not seen him for a few weeks — it was about a three-hour drive from home — sex was, of course, expected. My desire for him and for sex had only diminished further in the preceding months, as I wracked my brain trying to come up with a way to leave him without putting myself in danger. I stepped into the studio apartment he shared with another guy. They rented it for the summer while they both were enrolled in the program. It was like a dark, dank, unkempt trailer from the 1970s. I was grossed out just being in there. He pointed to the bed, and my stomach rolled. All I wanted was to go home and shower.

If the April incident was hell, this was the far-worse ninth ring thereof. He had purchased a Polaroid camera and insisted I pose for him naked while he clicked away. I flatly refused. I didn't even like seeing my own naked body in the mirror, and he knew that. Mostly, it was because of all the bullshit he spewed about my appearance. But I should have known that arguing was futile. He held all the power. Looking back, I can't believe how weak I was. It's like I was someone else entirely, because I never would tolerate such ridiculous, unacceptable behavior from anyone before or since. Back then, I grasped at straws.

"Well, you have a roommate, so, we really shouldn't," I said desperately.

"Don't worry about it; he's in class for the next few hours," he assured me. I tried praying silently but was so distraught and distracted I couldn't even think of the words to any prayers. Before I knew what was happening, my shorts and panties were on the floor and he was click-click-clicking away with the Polaroid. I tried frantically to ignore the flash. I tried to sit up, but he put his hand on my abdomen and held me down. The TV was on. I don't know what I was watching, but I watched as though my life depended on it, dying to be distracted from what was happening to me. I tried to cover myself, but he pushed my hands away. He made lewd comments and noises, and referred to certain parts of my womanhood with crude words. He touched me and clicked away. I wanted to vomit. I have never felt such fear, disgust and shame in my life. When he was finished, he insisted I look at the photos. I didn't want to. But before I knew it, I was looking at a shell of myself. There was a girl in the photos, looking at the TV with my face but no soul. She looked defeated. Her eyes were dead. She was incredibly thin. Who was this girl? Who was I? I didn't know anymore, but I was bound and determined to find out and get her out of that relationship while she was still alive. Her dignity, sense of self and pride were in shreds, but they were still there. I was determined to salvage them before it was too late.

I eventually did succeed in leaving him, but not without all the drama I'd feared. He had a gun on campus and threatened not only me but also my father's life. "I can't be responsible for my actions if I see you with someone else," he told me. A few months and an order of protection later, he graduated and left town.

To this day, I still struggle with rebuilding my life, myself, my self-confidence and my sex drive. But in time, I will be whole again. Of this I am sure.

A forgettable night

I was immediately attracted to him. He was tall and well built, and had dark hair and eyes. He was confident — not cocky — and charismatic.

This is as much as my memory can dredge up. I don't remember his name or where he came from. I knew little about him then and even less today.

Our acquaintance was brief. He came to the Naval base with a visiting squadron. He was part of one of the many flight exercises the base hosted.

I forgot exactly how we met, but we did. We hung out one night and had a rather enjoyable evening. We agreed to another night out.

I was excited by the prospect of new love, even though I knew he wouldn't be around long.

That Friday night, we met some of my friends at the enlisted club. We made our way to the bar and ordered cocktails; I probably had either a Seven & 7, rum and Coke with a splash of grenadine, or a white Russian — those were my drinks of choice back then. We sat with my friends and consumed our drinks before heading off as a group to the dance floor.

The sights and sounds began to blur. I felt strange.

Time passed without memory.

One minute, I was enjoying myself at the club, the next I was in a dark room. I was in a bed and my date was on top of me.

I blacked out.

When I opened my eyes, he still was on top of me, having sex with me.

Was I awake? Dreaming?

As I began to realize I was conscious and my vision started to focus in the darkness, I could see that it wasn't my date. It was someone else!

The moment I could muster any vocal capability, I screamed. The man jumped off of me and ran out the door.

I sat up and looked around the room. Where was I? Where was my date? Who was that man? What the hell was going on?!

I found my clothes on the floor, next to the bed. I grabbed them and put them on as quickly as I could. I surmised that I might be in my date's barracks room.

I opened the door and stepped into the common area; no one was around. I hung my head low in a tortuous walk of shame. I was confused.

I arrived at my barracks, opened the door, went to the

bathroom, and ran into the shower. I tried to scrub off what had happened, but it didn't work. I felt dirty.

All I could do afterward was to crawl in bed and hide there for the rest of the day.

I didn't hear from my date — at all. You'd think he would at least have called to explain where he'd gone and how I ended up with someone else in his room, or maybe to see if I was OK.

I did, however, run into one of his friends a couple of days later.

I was going to ignore him, but he insisted I talk to him.

"What, is he going to explain his friend's actions to me?" I thought. Weak.

He was nervous. I couldn't understand why.

When he opened his mouth, he apologized for having sex with me that night.

What? Did I hear him right?

He explained that he and a third man shared the barracks room with my date. When they came home that night and discovered us in the room, they sat outside in the common area. My date stepped out — after he had finished with me — and told them, "I've got one in there for you."

This man looked at the ground as he further explained that he went first and, when he was done, sent the third guy in. All three of them, he said, had sex with me while I was out cold. I woke up on the third one.

He showed remorse for his actions, but I couldn't forgive him — not yet, anyway.

Despite my growing fury, I didn't report the incident. For one, I didn't trust the base commanders, all men, to seek justice. Then, there was the fact that I had blacked out.

I knew the moment that I mentioned I had had a drink, I would have been put on trial for being a "drunk whore." They would have said that I consented during a night of drunken folly.

It was tough enough being a woman in the military; reporting any type of sexual assault or harassment would have made it worse. I just didn't have it in me to pursue it.

So, I kept my mouth shut, telling no one for many years.

Today, I wish I had had the courage to do what was right back then. Perhaps by making it public, our youngest generation of servicewomen would be safer, or at least feel like they could come forward without retaliation or judgment.

It's one of the few regrets I have.

When I finally opened up about my experience, a girlfriend asked me how I dealt with it. For years, I didn't. It manifested, like most traumas in life, into self-destructive behavior.

One day I realized that there were two kinds of people in the world — victims and survivors. I had played the victim long enough. I wanted to be a survivor.

I have a quote by Benjamin Franklin taped to my wall that I read every day.

"While we may not be able to control all that happens to us, we can control what happens inside us."

Those men took my body; that's all — mere flesh. They did not take my soul.

I live. I love. I feel compassion. I laugh. I forgive.

They have no power over me because I don't let them own me emotionally.

Those three men and, what they did to me, have faded away in the light of day.

Part IV:
Who we are

Independent bliss

By Ashley M. Ratcliff

There's something about the calm that overcomes your mind as you wash the dishes that have piled up during a week's worth of stressing, late nights on the clock and perfecting concoctions that loosely resemble "dinner."

Sometimes silence does more than any words can to let you know that everything is going to be all right. Now that I'm out living on my own, I am left with my thoughts and can loudly hear what speaks to my heart. I am alone but not lonely. Tired but not broken. Together, yet in complete disarray. Simultaneously satisfied and longing for what life has in store for me. I am doing things the way I want to, and I wouldn't have it any other way.

For me, adulthood/womanhood and independence/freedom have become synonymous. It's no multimillion-dollar, downtown penthouse, but my modest, one-bedroom apartment affords me all the independence I need. Imagine the joy that I (back then, a 22-year-old fresh out of college, claiming that fabled "oyster") experienced while hunting for the perfect spot, albeit in a new city, then paying the security deposit and first month's rent on my own. What seems like a small victory to some was a major accomplishment for me.

I'm fending for myself and I'm doing a pretty fine job. Taking the trash out? No problem. Scrubbing the toilet bowl? Somebody's got to do it. Mailing in that rent check — although it's about half of my monthly earnings (welcome to Los Angeles) — and bill payments are things I'm proud to do without relying on my parents or a man to keep me afloat. I am a grown woman.

At first, it was the simple manifestations of freedom that made me feel like I arrived at adulthood. I can eat ice cream straight out of the carton, dance around in my skivvies, entertain guests whenever I like, play my music as loud as I want, and sleep in as long as I please.

My apartment is all mine. No roommates, unless you consider that four-legged little boy: Berkeley Buster, my miniature Doberman-mix. I have earned the privilege of being selfish through surviving four tumultuous years of living cost-effectively and sharing a bedroom during college. And boy, do I have many a horror story to tell.

There was the one roommate who wasn't too keen on cleanliness. Her bodily stench alone literally made me nauseous, and I couldn't bring myself to explain to her that leaving a soiled

STORIES 4 WOMEN | 77

maxi pad attached to her underwear in plain view in our shoebox of a dorm room was a no-no.

Not to be outdone by this one, there was the inconsiderate roommate who thought she was allowed to use *my* ceramic bowl after a wild, drunken night to scoop her vomit out of the clogged toilet. She then proceeded to throw the dish in the trashcan. That same girl couldn't understand my outrage when my friend, visiting from out of town, found a used condom in her duffel bag — a souvenir from my roommate and her boyfriend's risqué rendezvous earlier that day. Gag.

I'd rather take 100 years of solitude than live through any of that nonsense again.

Then, the time came for me to step out onto life's next plateau when I earned my degree. There was the initial allure of my parents' house, where I could, essentially, revert back to my childhood, when a lot of things were handed to me: home-cooked meals, laundry, and rent- and bill-free living. But then, the realization that I would be "under their roof" again made me determined not to go back there for good. Heaven forbid I return to that safe space and lose my zeal for finding the perfect job or attaining future aspirations that become the benchmark of post-collegiate success. What? Throw away my freedom? No, thank you.

Don't get me wrong. My parents still act as a support system for me. By no means did I get to where I am today without their help, and they always are there for me when I need them.

I guess you can say that once I graduated from the university,

I graduated into real life — benefits, a 401(k) and all. I'm discovering who I am in my own space and growing on my own terms.

Sometimes I still eat like a college student, dress like a tomboy, daydream like a schoolgirl and, on a bad day, pout like that kid in the candy aisle who so desperately wants what she can't have. And I'm OK with that.

Independence sometimes isn't so glamorous to this single, 25-year-old woman. Dealing with car trouble; the dreaded mice, bugs and bumps in the night; those jars of spaghetti sauce that are screwed on too tight; and objects that require heavy lifting are just a few hurdles that, at times, make me consider running back to my safety net. But I stand my ground and chalk these scenarios up to building character. I just know that these experiences are making me stronger for when I progress in life, get married, and raise a family.

I'm constantly evolving while I'm pressing toward my dreams. Aside from my living arrangements and physical possessions, advancing to womanhood also is evident in my thought patterns and how I handle my emotions. By all means, cry. Let the tears flow. Scream into a pillow if you have to. Just don't take the problem out on others or place the blame elsewhere. It's about being accountable for your actions, recognizing when you're wrong, and caring enough to genuinely say, "I'm sorry." Not being scared to venture out by oneself is a feature of a strong individual.

In the romance department, I've learned that it's perfectly

fine to be single. But don't be afraid to take a chance on that special someone — it's worth the risk of getting your heart broken. Believe me, I'm still picking up the shattered scraps from the collapse of my first serious relationship.

At times when I'm down or think I've had all that I can handle, a wise friend or seasoned relative will remind me that, "The best is yet to come." I sigh and, when the idea registers, think, "Bring it on."

Making two worlds one

By Rebecca Villaneda

"Warning: Educated Latina." I saw that phrase on a purse a few years ago; my friend, Mayra, took a picture of a young woman holding it at the first May Day March in 2006. Many Mexican-Americans took to the streets to make clear the hard work they put in each day in California.

It's a bittersweet message to me that Latinas have to announce and prove that we've come this far.

I'm very proud to be Mexican-American, and even more proud of the strides my parents took to start a new life in a foreign country.

I grew up knowing our family was from Mexico, but I didn't grow up learning our culture. It was the way my parents wanted it, for their children to assimilate and respect the country that they moved to: respect the language, and America's culture and history.

I didn't question my parents' reasons. But I regret that I didn't do some investigating on my own.

I have a beautiful extended family back in Mexico; many of them I have never met, others just once or twice. Both my parents came from large families, and I have many *tias* (aunts) and *tios* (uncles) — some in their 80s and one in her 90s.

I love that I have such a rich history in Mexico; I just wish I knew more of it. I hear stories now and then, but there is so much to uncover that I hope to one day discover.

But until then, here I am — a minority in America and a female — a double whammy. I admit that I, thankfully, never have been judged or treated differently for being a Mexican or a female, but I see it around me constantly.

I've never had to feel embarrassed for being Mexican; maybe because I am one of those "educated Latinas," but I cringe at the unjust treatment other Mexicans living in America have to endure.

The stereotypes many Latino men and women face make me sad.

They are the dishwashers, the nannies, and the gardeners — all these hard jobs that no one else wants to take, yet they're viewed as lazy, uneducated, and here illegally.

And again, while I've never been judged for being a Latina, those are my people, so, of course, I'm going to be insulted at their mistreatment.

True, every ethnicity deals with its own stereotypes, but what good are they doing? They only segregate people more.

I met and interviewed Chicana activist Dolores Huerta, who walked side by side with Cesar Chavez during the grape farmworkers' strike in California in 1966. I'll never forget what she said to an auditorium of eager ears. Huerta said that cracking jokes about stereotypes, whether we believe in the prejudices or not, perpetuates the message, and that is part of the problem — not the solution.

That message hit my heart, and I've tried to apply it to everyday situations.

It's also hard to know that such a large percentage of young men join gangs because it's hard for them to be accepted into society.

My sister Liz a teacher, works with Latino kids in the Orange School District, in Orange County, California. Many of them drop out of school and don't think college is an option.

She explained the Advancement Via Individual Determination, or AVID, program that she recently joined, which helps students who otherwise wouldn't have a chance to prepare for college after high school. AVID helps students to realize their potential and shows them that they can be who and do anything they want to. One young Latina student said she wanted to be a judge but cowered at the thought, saying there was no such thing as a Latina judge. A teacher made the extra effort to introduce her to a prominent Latina judge, and she was so inspired.

Another little boy had never been to a ballgame before, and

someone cared enough to take him to one. Wide-eyed, he looked across the stadium and said, "I didn't know the world was this big."

Small things like that change people's perspectives. A little attention goes a long way.

Children, like the two I just described, number in the thousands. Their parents may be too poor to show them otherwise, but they had enough drive, like my parents, to find opportunity in a grand country. There's enough prospect in America; the stifling stereotypes are unnecessary.

It's unfair to have these typecasts of a people and the Mexico I know and love — especially the parts my family is from — with cobblestone streets, elegant architecture, vibrant colors, greeting smiles left and right. That is a far cry from the negative depictions in America.

In the midst of this, I struggle with trying to be true to my heritage yet staying faithful to my country.

It's hard that I grew up American and lost my Mexican identity in the meantime. My niece Anna asked me if I had a *quinceñeara*. No, I didn't, and neither did my two sisters, Liz and Ruthie. We didn't have a Sweet 16 either.

I am grateful to be an American, where we, as a people, are lucky to live with freedom of choice, a safe infrastructure, and a government that is, for the most part, not corrupt.

However, I'm disappointed in myself for not knowing more about my Mexican culture and its holidays. My Spanish isn't terrific, either; I can hold a decent conversation and I can get my point across in a letter, but being that I am only a first-generation American, it should be a lot cleaner.

In the movie "Selena," starring Jennifer Lopez, I'll never forget the scene where her father, played by Edward James Olmos, said, "It's hard being Mexican-American. You have to know who Cristina and Oprah is."

It's true. I let down my fellow *Mexicanas* if I don't know a certain word in Spanish, and if an English-speaking friend asks me a question about Mexico or a Spanish word, I feel pressure to know the answer.

My family members in Mexico — they don't mean to give me a hard time — laugh because my favorite adjective is *bonito*, or beautiful.

But ask me to describe something in English, and I'll come up with something more creative than "beautiful."

It's a constant battle, but one I've accepted as a work in progress. After all, an educated Latina never stops learning.

Journey to 'ever after'

By Amy Higgins Artino

Trying to sleep last night was like trying to drowse on Christmas Eve when you're 6 years old, only even harder.

I woke up groggy but excited this morning, and rolled over to see my cousin and bridesmaid Ashlee still sound asleep. I got up so as not to disturb her and ran downstairs to eat breakfast with the family. I could hear that my parents, and another cousin and bridesmaid, Kate, were awake, as was my sister and maid of honor, Sara.

Dad had sliced fresh peaches for me in the hopes that I would be able to eat despite my raging nerves. I told him he didn't have to cut them for me, but he insisted. It was his last chance to "take care of his princess before she became someone else's" today. It simultaneously warmed and broke my heart. The peaches were like liquid sugar.

I paced all morning until the hairstylist came. She set my tresses in hot rollers while we made small talk, and I couldn't help but notice how thick her Philadelphia accent was; clearly I'd been living away from home longer than I thought. My mind wandered to the incensed storm in my head and stomach, seizing my lungs, shaking my limbs.

I heard my missing bridesmaid, Lisa, come in. She had been here before to drop off hairstyling paraphernalia but headed back out to put gas in her car. Her musical, carefree laugh, never frazzled and always welcoming, made me feel even more fidgety and out of control.

I walked down the stairs thinking I must have looked like Medusa with my hair rolled that way, and the Earth-angel who served as our wedding coordinator for the day was in the kitchen. I was elated to see her. Just being in her presence had a calming effect. I felt like I was suffering from the worst case of stage fright I'd ever had: In just a few short hours, I would be Mike's wife. I was overjoyed at the thought — but getting to that point, with hundreds of eyes staring at me as I tried not to trip, as I was put on display throughout the entire Mass, was more than putting me on edge.

Somehow, somewhere in the midst of the waltz that was everyone's concurrent dressing routine, a sandwich platter arrived. I was too nervous to eat but afraid of fainting at the altar if I didn't, so I chewed thoughtlessly and made more small talk. The food was like lead in my mouth, pulling uncomfortably at my stomach with a tenuous, invisible string.

I tried to talk to the girls about what was new in their lives, desperate for a distraction.

Between the time my last bridesmaid, Mary — also awash in hot rollers — showed up, and Lisa and Kate had their hair beautifully coifed in place, the clock had grown a mind of its own. The hours between 10 a.m. and noon had simply vanished into thin air, never stopping once to account for themselves. The photographer was coming at 2 p.m., as were the flowers, and not long after that, the limo would come to whisk us away to the church as I grasped onto the last remaining moments of my life as a bachelorette. It wasn't that I was going to miss being single — it was my ever-present fear of change and nostalgia for one chapter of my life as it faded into another. I tried to savor it all in the short time I had left.

Before I knew it, my hair had been sculpted into a curl-laden masterpiece with the veil in place, the florist was ringing the doorbell, and I was scratching and clawing at the last shreds of my sanity.

What if his wedding party members are incredibly late? What if the priest — since he is new — forgets some major part of the sacrament? What if I'm an inconsolable mess of nerves and tulle and can't do all that I'm supposed to? What if, God forbid, someone has the indecency to clear his or her throat when the priest asks if anyone objects to our union?

"What God has joined together, let no man put asunder," I thought to myself over and over. And shame on anyone who tried.

I had a vision in my mind for the flowers throughout the yearlong planning process, but nothing could have prepared me for the exquisite showpieces being paraded into the house. They were less like flowers and more like inimitable jewels, in all shades of fuschia, amethyst, chartreuse and orange. I was blown away. I had just enough time to thank the florist before Sara and my bridesmaids, with the help of my mother, had me zipped up into the gown of my dreams. I walked past the mirror, caught a glimpse and was stunned. Who was that staring back at me with my eyes, my face, in such ethereal regalia? My father walked into the room just then and looked at me. His face turned red, his eyes welled up and that's when the first of my tears came. I told him to take no offense if I didn't look at him — I had to keep my makeup on as long as I could. He handed me a handkerchief from his drawer. It was white with a black "H" embroidered on it for "Higgins." He told me I could use it since my last initial wouldn't be "H" after today. That feeling returned for what felt like the millionth time in months — the feeling that the "old me" was dying and a new stranger with someone else's name was taking her place, and that I was willingly leaving my parents bereft of their first-born daughter.

The photo session was the only part of the day that didn't go by in, ahem, a flash. I hate having my picture taken, but I knew I wanted as many memories of this day as I could have, so I acceded without complaint. I was willing to bet, though, that whatever expression showed on my face had no resemblance to the tumult going on inside of me. I just wanted to get to the church to see Mike. It had been a mere 12 hours since we had seen each other last, but it felt like days. Besides, the buildup was threatening to kill me.

It wasn't the union itself that destroyed my composure so much as everything leading up to it: The parade down the aisle while everyone inspected me with a mental fine-toothed comb; the war against the tears that refused to stay put deep inside my tear ducts, where they belonged; the heartbreaking, ritualistic kiss goodbye to my father; the stumbling my way through my vows as said tears ravaged my voice. The groom awaiting my arrival at the altar, Mr. Somewhat-Tall-but-Dark-and-Handsome — the one who shares my hopes and dreams, my laughter and pain, my joys and fears — was the one unwavering article of serenity within the entire ceremony, the light at the end of the flower-laden tunnel.

Once in the limo with my maids and my parents, the disquietude kicked into overdrive. Dad fooled with the radio, looking for a station that would be agreeable to everyone, while my eyes darted around the interior, watching as the neon lights flashed in time to the music, aware that only my heart was pulsating faster than they were.

We got to the church and sneaked in the side entrance to the Infant of Prague Room, which served as the bridal chamber where we all would wait for the ceremony to begin. I lingered in the hall outside the door by myself so I could collect my thoughts and emotions, both of which continued to elude me. After a few minutes, sweet Diane, one of the onsite coordinators, came around the corner and gasped, telling me how beautiful I looked and asking me how I felt. My voice cracked and tears spilled over as I confessed, "I'm really nervous." She said a prayer over me and I felt a little more composed.

I went into the room to be with the rest of my loved ones in the wedding party. I couldn't stop crying. The angelic, radiant sounds emanating from the violin and piano in the church didn't help. Dad held my hands and asked me what was wrong. I just shook and cried and assured him I wasn't unhappy, just overwhelmed — and shattered over being responsible for him "losing" his daughter to someone else.

Tim, the photographer, came into the room then and jokingly asked if the Infant of Prague was there. We all cracked up. Overcome by nerves and the sound of my stomach growling, I said the first thing that came to mind: "He was here — but we ate him." We all laughed again as I wondered where in my disordered brain such a senseless comment came from. My bouquet shook like a maraca in my hands.

Before I knew what was happening next, we were all lined up in the tiny, narrow hallway, each awaiting our turn to process down the aisle. Sara pulled the blusher over my face and adjusted the veil in the back while we simultaneously, ever mentally connected, made a reference to a creepy, memorable scene in the movie "The Others." My laughter was genuine and it felt exhilarating, but threatened to border on hysterics.

Soon, it was just Dad and I waiting for our cue, while the blood in my head played a drum solo to rival the one from Phil Collins' "In the Air Tonight." Dad looked so handsome in his tux, his face both elated and aggrieved, wise and innocent. I put my right arm through his left one, we walked to the double doors and he asked, "Are you ready?" I took a deep breath, listened to the swelling strains of the violin and nodded once. The doors opened. I looked ahead, smiling and crying, and saw my groom. He, too, was grinning through tears. I knew I was more than ready; I had waited for this day throughout my entire existence. Dad and I took one step forward on the journey to the rest of my life.

The agony of aging, the thrill of defeating it

By Mary Scott

Oh Lord! I hate looking in the mirror.

It's not even cliché anymore. It's a theme song for many women growing older: "I don't recognize the face staring back at me."

My first gray hair came in when I was 21 years old, and it has come in steadily every year since. However, in the last year, the gray seems to have gone through a growth spurt — the taunting white buggers tripling in number every time I have to color. I'm now sporting gray at the temples and down along the sides. My left part is completely silver, and white streaks are popping up in the front.

As I try to stomach getting ready in the morning, there is nothing I can see in that reflective glass that resembles me anymore. My face is covered with splotches from a crazy, mid-

30s battle with adult acne. My eyelids are getting droopy, making me look tired all the time. The skin between my eyebrows creases deeply into my skull. The laugh lines around my mouth look like a set of parenthesis and the worst part, I have a jowl. I have a *jowl*!

It's not just my face, either. My butt is bigger, my belly bulges over my pants and it has been a long time since I've had a waistline.

Even my boobs have gotten bigger. Go figure why that couldn't have happened to me in my 20s! And before you start thinking, "Why is she complaining about bigger boobs?" let me say just one thing: sagging skin.

I remember when in my teenage years and even into my 20s, if I needed to drop some weight, I could do so in a matter of days. One three-day fad diet and I was 10 pounds lighter. Now, I can only drop 10 pounds after months and months of strenuous effort.

There isn't an inch on my face or body that hasn't gone through some sort of horrid metamorphosis.

Getting older wouldn't bother me so much if I didn't feel young still. I'm 45 but I feel more like 30 — well ... OK, 35. I certainly still live like I'm younger: I rent, I have no children, no retirement account, and little savings. And, I've been told that I don't act my age.

Of course, I am about to be married — for the second time.

Oh dear! Why don't I look like a blushing bride-to-be?

A bride at midlife — how 21st century. Can one plan a wedding and have a midlife crisis at the same time?

I totally get that whole midlife *thing* now. Ten years ago, I thought men's and women's desperation to retain their youth as long as possible was completely ridiculous. Now I understand.

Reaching the middle of your life is hard. You're too young to feel old and too old to be young.

It wasn't that long ago that I could walk into a nightclub and still blend. Now I feel like the crowd is whispering, "What's the old lady doing in here?"

It seems like yesterday that I was in Richmond, Kentucky, playing quarters with some frat boys at a dark table in The Family Dog. Today, I'm just a few years away from AARP eligibility.

Though the discounts will be nice, I'm really not ready to have a Boy Scout escort me across the street so I won't be run over by passing motorists.

When I look in that mirror, I sigh and think, "What I wouldn't give to be in my 20s again."

Wait! I ponder that for a bit longer. I ask myself, "Why?"

My 20s were horrible. Sure, I was playing beer games with some hotties, but I also was drinking too much and skipping class because of hangovers.

I dropped out of college with a low grade-point average, and I was stupid, naïve, and had very low self-esteem.

I had dreams but I was too afraid to pursue them.

And as for the situations I got myself into, only the Great Spirit in the sky knows how I survived.

As I approached my mid-30s, I was tired of the crazy times. I thought it was time that I should settle down. So I got hitched to the next guy who came along. He was a decent and generous enough man; he just wasn't the right one for me.

By the time my 30s ended, I was divorced.

I certainly was not the person that the 11-year-old me wanted to be.

But maybe I wasn't supposed to be that person. Perhaps my destiny was to be someone different — the person I've become.

In my 40s, I finally have stepped on the right path and my real journey is just beginning. All that has led up to this point has been training. And I'm using everything I've learned.

I'm smarter and emotionally stronger.

You know the saying, "What doesn't kill you only makes you stronger." Well, if that's true, I'm the emotional equivalent of Mr. Universe.

I'm a better judge of people and situations, and I know who and what I can trust.

I can reach for the sky but know how to keep my feet planted on terra firma. I have the experience I need to follow my true passion.

So, I'll embrace my wrinkles. They represent all the laughter and fun, and the pain and tears — and the inquisitive expressions my friends have come to know me for — that I've had in my life.

I'll embrace my larger breasts, even if I have to pick them up off the ground to do so.

The gray hair — *well*, I'm still working on accepting that.

Today, I'll cover the mirror because, after all, it's not about how I look. It's about how I feel.